THE EAGLE RETURNS

THE EAGLE RETURNS

A Fresh Look at the Gospel of John

C. Paul Burnham

WIPF & STOCK · Eugene, Oregon

THE EAGLE RETURNS
A Fresh Look at the Gospel of John

Wipf & Stock
An Imprint of Wipf and Stock Publishers
199 W. 8th Ave., Suite 3
Eugene, OR 97401

www.wipfandstock.com

PAPERBACK ISBN: 978-1-5326-4200-5
HARDCOVER ISBN: 978-1-5326-4201-2
EBOOK ISBN: 978-1-5326-4202-9

Manufactured in the U.S.A.

To the memory of my brother

JOHN CLARK BURNHAM
1935–1946

whose illness and untimely death
first led me to read the Gospel of John

CONTENTS

Contents

Acknowledgments

Although this book is a personal testimony, I owe a huge debt to the late Professor Howard Marshall, my lifelong mentor in everything to do with the New Testament. I have also cherished an equally long friendship with Patrick and Ruth Edwards. Ruth's work on the Gospel of John opened my eyes to the wealth of academic studies on the subject. Howard and Ruth would have preferred the words "probably" and "perhaps" to figure more often in this book, but, nevertheless, they were both very helpful in its preparation. Dr. Ben Pugh, of Cliff College, encouraged me to offer it to Wipf and Stock for publication.

PART ONE

INTRODUCTION

1:1. The Objective of This Book

THE GOSPEL OF JOHN is unique in that it is an account of the life, teaching, death and resurrection of Jesus Christ which is not a collection of eyewitness memories edited by someone else, but claims to be written by an author who was himself an eyewitness. It includes theological discussions that have played a pivotal part in the development of creeds and other doctrinal literature throughout Christian history. John's Gospel was written with the express purpose of transforming the lives of its readers by bringing them to faith in Christ. Thus it can become a work of testimony at three levels, concerning the story of Jesus Christ, concerning the Evangelist as his own life was transformed, and concerning all those throughout history who have been brought to saving faith in Christ through the words of the Gospel of John. This three-level testimony is an important theme in what follows here. Sadly, during the last century, this edifice of faith has been undermined by scholars doubting whether John's Gospel really was the work of an eyewitness. Some have sought written sources, but without decisive results. An influential alternative was that it was the construct of a hypothetical "Johannine Community," and this has led to the creation of a mass of literature of little value to people seeking an encounter with the real Jesus Christ. The aim of this booklet is to explore the possibilities that open if its claim to be the work of one well-informed author is accepted. Then the gospel can used once more as a testimony to Jesus Christ as he really was in his ministry, to John Evangelist as a witness to him and to the truth that, when the Holy Spirit applies its words as people read the gospel, their lives can be transformed.

1:2. Attitudes to the Gospel of John

Many Christians in the English-speaking world found that Archbishop William Temple's *Readings in St. John's Gospel* opened a new window through which to perceive the unique greatness of Jesus Christ. In 1938 Temple could affirm that it was "vital to St. John's purpose that the events which he records should be actual events. We can be quite sure that he never consciously wrote what he did not believe to be fact. . . . We shall read the Gospel as valid history so far as its record of events is concerned."[1] Temple then affirms that "each conversation or discourse contained in the Gospel actually took place. But it is so reported as to convey, not only the sounds uttered or the meaning then apprehended, but the meaning which, always there, has been disclosed by lifelong meditation."[2]

Dorothy L. Sayers was a seasoned author and a formidable scholar, who wore out her Greek New Testament in writing her radio play cycle *The Man Born to Be King*, published in 1943. She testified in the introduction that "it must be remembered that, of the four Evangels St. John's is the only one that claims to be the direct report of an eye-witness. And to anyone accustomed to the imaginative handling of documents, the internal evidence bears out this claim,"[3] . . . "it reads like the narrative of an eye-witness, filling up the gaps in material already published, correcting occasional errors and adding material which previous writers either

---

1. Temple, *Readings in St. John's Gospel*, xiii.
2. Ibid., xviii.
3. Sayers, *Man Born to Be King*, 33.

had not remembered or did not know about."[4] . . . "It is, generally speaking, John who knows the time of year, the time of day, where people sat and how they got from one place to another."[5]

But already by this time, it was a commonplace of scholarship to question the gospel's historical reliability as an account of the life and teaching of Jesus. Twentieth-century literature has been reviewed (with about 450 references) by Ruth Edwards.[6] She points out that many scholars have supposed that John's "beloved disciple" is not a real historical person at all, but a literary fiction.[7] She also comments on the influence of sociological theory and social-scientific analysis on Johannine interpretation which has "led to a widespread hypothesis that John stems from a small community with a 'sectarian' outlook, locked in bitter conflict with the Jewish Synagogue. . . . This hypothesis has become so popular that it is often simply assumed."[8] Yet it stands in total contrast with the earlier view that John's Gospel was obviously written by one well-informed author. Careful evaluation of the evidence led Edwards to conclude that "the scholarly construct of John writing from, and for, a small and isolated community with narrow sectarian views should certainly be rejected. The gospel would have been produced in the context of a believing community, but there is no need to suppose that it was written exclusively for this group.". . . "John intended his Gospel for a wide audience, including Jews, Jewish Christians, Gentiles, Gentile Christians, and, conceivably, Samaritans."[9]

The last decade has seen a powerful reaffirmation of the historical reliability of the gospels in general, and John's Gospel in particular, most notably by Richard Bauckham. The general theme was set in a book entitled *Jesus and the Eyewitnesses*, published in 2006, with a revised edition in 2017. Bauckham presented a

4. Ibid., 34.

5 Ibid., 33.

6. Edwards, *Discovering John* (1st ed.).

7. Ibid., 19.

8. Ibid., 15.

9. Ibid., 44.

persuasive case that the preferred source for the constituent materials of the gospels was eyewitness testimony. In the case of the Synoptics, separate nuggets of remembered information (*pericopes*) were strung together by editors who were not themselves eyewitnesses. With the exception of the last week, where their narratives become more continuous, these editors had no access to a biographical framework of the life of Jesus. A few items, such as those relating to John the Baptist, the temptations, and the call of the core Galilean disciples, obviously belonged to the beginning of his public ministry. Everything else was arranged around a simple pattern of a ministry in Galilee, one journey to Jerusalem with various incidents on the way and, at the end, one stay of barely a week in or near Jerusalem.

Even without reference to the Gospel of John, there is compelling evidence that the full story of the life of Jesus was much more complex, including, for example, a more extensive ministry in Jerusalem. The clearest indication is in Luke 13:34–35 (also Matt 23:37), "Jerusalem . . . *how often* I have longed to gather your children together." This is also a good example of a pericope placed at a different point in the story by two synoptic writers. Making a base at Bethany (Mark 11:1; 14:3–9) suggests previous hospitality there, as is implied by Luke (10:38–42). Finally, the rapid establishment of a substantial Christian community in Jerusalem, including members of the Jewish establishment (Acts 6:7), would strain credulity if Jesus had been a stranger there before Palm Sunday. The unfamiliarity of the Synoptic editors with his activities in Jerusalem was pungently exposed by J. A. T. Robinson. They do not explain the faith of people like Joseph of Arimathea or the "man, whose very name they fail to give, who is so loyal in his faith that in his darkest hour he will keep an upper room ready for Him."[10] But "while the Johannine chronology cannot be fitted into the Markan because the latter is fragmentary, the Markan can be fitted into the Johannine."[11] The review of John's Gospel below shows how this can be achieved.

10. Robinson, *Priority of John*, 125–26.

11. Ibid., 124.

1:3. The Nature of the Gospel of John

The declared origin of John's Gospel differs from the Synoptics. Their compilers would all doubtless claim that they were based on the testimony of eyewitnesses, as Luke does explicitly (1:1–4). But John's Gospel claims that its contents were actually written down by an eyewitness (21:24). The opening paragraph of the First Letter of John (1 John 1:1–5) may well refer to the writing of the gospel. "That . . . which we have heard, which we have seen with our eyes . . . we proclaim concerning the Word of Life." This very significant passage has been discussed by John Stott.[12] Stott argues strongly for common authorship of the letters of John and the gospel, a view supported by Martin Hengel and Howard Marshall.[13] In keeping with authorship by an eyewitness, John's Gospel is a continuous narrative with few instances of pericopes. It was clearly intended to be chronological, and was well supplied with topographical indications of a number of journeys. After much careful consideration, Richard Bauckham was persuaded that the traditional view of the gospel is correct. In *The Testimony of the Beloved Disciple*, he states "In my view, the Gospel is an integral whole, including both the prologue and the epilogue, and was designed as such by a single author."[14] The evidence is that "no parts of the Gospel are stylistically distinguishable from others."[15] Bauckham further claims that "the Gospel of John . . . is, as it stands, the way one eyewitness understood what he and others had seen."[16] This is, of course, disputed by many other authorities, most spectacularly by Geza Vermes. "The total irreconcilability of the Fourth Gospel with the Synoptics combined with the late date of its composition would strongly militate against an author who was an eyewitness

12. Stott, *Letters of John*, 30–37.

13. Ibid., 20–28; Hengel, *Johannine Question*, 176–77; Marshall, *New Testament Theology*, 29.

14. Bauckham, *Testimony of the Beloved Disciple*, 12.

15. Ibid., 30.

16. Bauckham, *Jesus and the Eyewitnesses*, 411.

of the historical Jesus."[17] However, Edwards is confident that the Gospel of John was in or near its present form not later than 100 CE, and possibly as early as 70–80 CE,[18] when a youthful eyewitness might still be living. The case that the content of the gospel complements the Synoptic accounts, and is not incompatible with them, is presented in part 2 of this book.

It is right to be cautious about claims to eyewitness testimony (e.g., concerning 2 Pet 1:16–18). But it is perverse to reject them out of hand, as many have done in the case of John's Gospel. This book is an examination of the implications of accepting not merely that it contains elements derived from the memories of an eyewitness, but that the episodes that are described in detail are those where the author or someone known to him was present, and that matters outside such personal experience are omitted or passed over very briefly. The Evangelist himself was well aware of this selectivity (20:30; 21:25). It is accepted that he saw everything through the lens of his theological beliefs, although these too were molded by his experience of the words and works of Jesus. So history passed sometimes into theological commentary. No doubt the passage of time meant that he provided exact wording for conversations which he remembered only in outline. This was an accepted practice in ancient historiography.[19] But I do John the Evangelist the honor of believing that when he records events or conversations, something of the sort did happen. The hypothesis that the Evangelist's memories, mutated inevitably by thinking about them in the light of later experiences, were the predominant source of his material, explains why it is so difficult to find evidence of other sources. The peculiar periphrases whereby I am supposing he identifies himself without giving a name, such as "the disciple whom Jesus loved," seemed appropriate to the Evangelist, however peculiar they seem to us. In the case of the second disciple who accompanied Andrew in 1:35–51, it presumably seemed too early

17. Vermes, *Changing Faces of Jesus*, 10.

18. Edwards, *Discovering John*, 57.

19. Bauckham, *Testimony of the Beloved Disciple*, 106–12.

in his acquaintance with Jesus to use this phrase, but the detailed conversations recorded suggest that this too was the Evangelist.

1:4. Who Was John the Evangelist?

Traditionally he was identified with John bar Zebedee, the fisherman, who was brother to James. The grounds for this are given, for example, by Bruce Milne.[20] It is argued that only the Twelve were present at the "Last Supper." This is said to be evidenced by Mark 14:17, which states that "Jesus arrived with the Twelve." This book follows Bauckham in proposing that the Evangelist was not John bar Zebedee, who indeed arrived with the Twelve.[21] It is proposed that John Evangelist was the householder, and so already present. At the supper he would then have the place of honor, next to Jesus, because he was the host. He was thus able to hear every word of Jesus' farewell discourse, which he recorded in such detail in his gospel. He was possibly the only Jerusalem disciple present. In contrast, John bar Zebedee was a Galilean, and a leading member of the Twelve. Surely it is inconceivable that he could have sponsored a gospel with such a limited coverage of the Galilean ministry of Jesus, and so little mention of the Twelve. There is no mention of the special occasions, such as the Transfiguration, the raising of Jairus's daughter or the agony in the Garden of Gethsemane, where John bar Zebedee was one of the three privileged witnesses. Moreover, the limited education (Acts 4:13) and the impulsive character of John bar Zebedee (Mark 10:35–45; Luke 9:54) were in total contrast to the Evangelist, who, even in youth, was surely thoughtful, well educated and theologically sophisticated. He writes of the activities of the religious establishment of Jerusalem as an "insider." If he was the unnamed disciple of 18:15, he was well known to Annas, the high priest emeritus. Bizarrely, it has been supposed that John bar Zebedee was "known to the high priest" because he

---

20. Milne, *Message of John*, 15–19.

21. Bauckham, *Testimony of the Beloved Disciple*, 15.

supplied fish to his household.[22] But Barrett interprets the phrase as meaning a close friend or relative.[23] So the unnamed disciple must have been a member of the religious establishment in Jerusalem. As Bauckham rightly urges, with these and other arguments, "the old attribution to John the son of Zebedee . . . is a phantom that needs to be finally and completely exorcised."[24]

It is important to remember that John was one of the commonest names among first-century Palestinian Jews.[25] The example of the two Philips shows how readily subsequent authors conflate people with the same name. It is therefore easy to understand why Christian authors, from the second century onward, presumed that so well informed an author must have been one of the Twelve, who were appointed by Jesus to be with him in Galilee. The contrary view, expressed by Bauckham,[26] is that John the Evangelist was a resident of Jerusalem. Nevertheless he was a disciple, first of John the Baptist and then of Jesus. He had a substantial house in Jerusalem, which enabled him to offer a home to the mother of Jesus. It is noteworthy that most of the gospel is concerned with events that are located in or near Jerusalem, in very marked contrast to the Synoptics.

In later life, the Evangelist may have been John the Elder, of Ephesus,[27] a possibility explored in a following section. In youth, he could have been a protégé of Nicodemus, an influential Pharisee, who features prominently on three occasions in the gospel, but nowhere else in the New Testament. Bauckham believes that the Gurion family, to which Nicodemus almost certainly belonged, had a country estate near Cana in Galilee.[28] It would be neat to suppose that John Evangelist was a pupil of Nicodemus, as Paul

22. Brownrigg, *Who's Who in the New Testament*, 283.

23. Barrett, *Gospel according to St. John*, 525–26.

24. Bauckham, *Testimony of the Beloved Disciple*, 75. Ruth Edwards agrees. Her arguments are set out in *Discovering John* (2nd ed.), 28–30.

25. Bauckham, *Testimony of the Beloved Disciple*, 15.

26. Ibid., 14–16.

27. Ibid., 50.

28. Ibid., 160.

was of Gamaliel. In this case, he might have found hospitality in Galilee, which would greatly ease making the extended visits that are suggested here. Cana is mentioned three times in the Gospel of John, but nowhere else in the Bible. But such ideas can be no more than interesting speculations.

1:5. The Approach of This Book

There are many scholarly commentaries on the Gospel of John. I have frequently consulted those by C. K. Barrett[29] and George R. Beasley-Murray.[30] But Barrett was committed to a skeptical viewpoint, and both gave most of their space to details, whereas my object is to evaluate an alternative "big picture." So what follows is not a detailed commentary, but a survey which explores the hypothesis that John the Evangelist wrote the gospel almost entirely on the basis of his own memories. Where he provided circumstantial detail or supplied conversations, it is assumed in this exercise that he, or an informant, was actually present at the time. It is further assumed that where an unnamed disciple took a considerable part in the incident, that disciple was the Evangelist himself.[31] One result of these assumptions is that the gospel becomes not only a biographical account of the ministry of Jesus, but also a spiritual autobiography of the Evangelist during the same period. The implications of this will also be considered in the course of this survey of his gospel. These assumptions cannot be proven, any more than the attitudes of a supposed "Johannine community" can be ascertained with certainty, but their implications can be explored and the result assessed. Problems will undoubtedly appear as a result.

But John Evangelist did not write his gospel to be picked over by scholars. He selected the material to form his picture of the words and works of Jesus so that ordinary people through the ages might believe his claim to be uniquely related to God,

29. Barrett, *Gospel according to St. John.*

30. Beasley-Murray, *John.*

31. This assumption has been challenged by Ruth Edwards, *Discovering John* (2nd ed.), 182–83. Of course, it cannot be proved one way or the other.

and trust their lives to him. It was written so that you, the reader, might "believe that Jesus is the Christ, the Son of God, and that by believing you may have life in His name" (20:21). The emphasis is in making an immediate commitment, the necessity for deciding here and now for "life" or "death." The offer is of eternal life, not only for the hereafter, but as an immediate transformation of the whole person. We read John's Gospel to meet Jesus, and to share what John Evangelist heard, what he saw with his eyes, what he looked at and what his hands touched concerning the Word of life. We read it to have fellowship with him and his fellow disciples, because their very lively fellowship was with God, the Father, and with his Son, Jesus Christ. We read it that joy, both theirs and ours, may be made complete (1 John 1:1–4). So, what follows is not intended to be read on its own, but as an accompaniment to reading the gospel itself.

PART TWO

A SURVEY OF THE GOSPEL OF JOHN

2:1. Our Place in the Big Picture (1:1–18)

MOST DISCUSSIONS ABOUT THIS prologue center on its theological statements, but its primary function was to introduce the gospel, its aims and major themes. It is to be about Jesus Christ. He was with God "in the beginning," but came into the world as a flesh-and-blood human being to make God known. From this it follows that a reliable record of his life and utterances is of immense importance. As William Temple wrote: "The Gospel is that the Word was made flesh, and being incarnate so spoke, so acted, so died and so rose from death." . . . "It is then vital to St. John's purpose that the events he records should be real events."[1]

At the same time, he was also God "the One and Only," fully associated with God "the Father" in his activity in creating and sustaining the universe. This is implied by the use of "Word" (*logos*), in a sense taken from Greek philosophy. But Jesus is not just "a Word" but "The Word" (*ho logos*). He is the One God in action and communication. His association with God is so strong that he does not negate the monotheism of the Old Testament. Richard Bauckham devoted a whole chapter to discussing this.[2] His mes-

1. Temple, *Readings in St. John's Gospel*, xiii.
2. "Monotheism and Christology in the Gospel of John," in Bauckham, *Testimony of the Beloved Disciple*, 239–52.

11

sage was for the world, but the gospel will tell of his rejection by many. But it will also tell of a community, to be called "the children of God," consisting of those who believed his claims. They will be uniquely blessed.

It is important to understand that it is not only the narrative parts of John's Gospel that are based on the memories of an eyewitness; the theological reflections are also derived from the remembered words of Jesus. Those in the prologue rest on the status claimed by Jesus, for example, "before Abraham was born, I AM," the Hebrew name for God (8:58). John's Gospel repeatedly makes it clear that Jesus claimed to speak with the voice of God (e.g., 8:28). Its challenge is for the reader to believe that he was, and is, who he claimed to be. In a traditional Church of England funeral, the priest leads in the casket with the words: "I am the Resurrection and the Life, saith the Lord. He that believeth in Me, though He were dead, yet shall He live: and whosoever liveth and believeth in Me shall never die." But that is not all that Jesus said to Martha (11:26). He followed with the question "Do you believe this?" This challenge confronts the reader in every part of John's Gospel, alongside the promise that, through believing, you will find life, indeed eternal life, through him.

2:2. First Encounter with Jesus in Galilee (1:19–51)

Following our hypothesis, John's account of the earthly life of Jesus does not begin with his birth and infancy, but at the point when the Evangelist first met him. It is tempting to suppose that John Evangelist was part of the group of religious leaders from Jerusalem, who visited John the Baptist. According to both Matthew (3:7) and John (1:24–5), this included some Pharisees, thus possibly including Nicodemus. But if the Evangelist was the unnamed disciple of John the Baptist (1:35–42), who was on easy terms with the Galilean Andrew, he must have been with the Baptist for some time. In this case, the memories recorded in vv. 19–34 could also be those of John Evangelist, including the Baptist's description of Jesus as "the Lamb of God who takes away the sin of the world."

Simon Peter was apparently also a fellow member of John the Baptist's entourage. Prompted by the Baptist's testimony, the three transferred their allegiance to Jesus at this point. We note that, if John Evangelist is accepted consistently as the unnamed disciple in John's Gospel, Simon Peter and John Evangelist become associated at the very beginning and again at the end, an *inclusio* pointed out by Bauckham.[3] An *inclusio* is like a pair of bookends, and suggests that what lies between has been planned as a unit. In any case John pictures Jesus having an informal group of accompanying disciples considerably before the ordination of the Twelve, and, granted the truth of our hypothesis, one of its members was John Evangelist. The detailed record of their first conversations surely reflects the significance of the episode as a milestone in John's own life, the birthplace of the deep allegiance to Jesus that was the mainspring of his subsequent career. In these conversations with Jesus we also see important truths about our relationship with Jesus. From the very beginning he knows all about us (1:47–48), and we sense that he is a special person, who has the right to command our allegiance (1:49). Beyond this, he is calling us to future experiences that will be truly awesome (1:50).

2:3. The Wedding at Cana (2:1–12)

Both the detail in the story and the significance given to the miracle are compelling evidence that John Evangelist was present at the wedding at Cana. Such a miracle presents a problem to modern minds, and it would be congenial to such if we could assume it was really a quick-witted kindness on the part of the Master of Ceremonies. My teetotal grandfather was wont to describe water as "Adam's Ale" or "Lions' Beer." But, in this case, it would in no way support the weight placed on it by the Evangelist. For him it is not only a confirmation that Jesus is possessed of powers of divine origin, but that he is worthy of the total trust of John and the other disciples. John's confidence in the God-given authority

---

3. Bauckham, *Gospel of Glory*, 131–84.

of Jesus really began here. Yet, Jesus himself felt that the use of his powers was premature while he was still subject to the loyalties of family life.

2:4. Jesus Begins His Ministry in Jerusalem (2:13–35)

Now Jesus left his family and traveled to Jerusalem for the feast of the Passover with a small group of disciples, which we assume included John Evangelist. His visit there began with the "Cleansing of the Temple." This is the subject of a pericope in the Gospels of Matthew (21:12–14), Mark (11:15–17) and Luke (19:45–46), who place it in the last week of his ministry. Matthew and Mark mention the use of the incident as evidence at the trial of Jesus before Caiaphas. Dorothy Sayers drew attention to the difficulty the witnesses found in agreeing the exact wording of the comment.[4] This is more plausible if the incident occurred two or three years previously, rather than earlier in the same week. Jesus' riposte about John the Baptist (Mark 11:29–33) would also make better sense at this time, rather than some time after the Baptist had been taken out of circulation by imprisonment and death. Robinson found evidence that the money changers' stalls were allowed only for the three weeks immediately previous to the Passover.[5] So an incident involving overturning them must be dated to an occasion when Jesus visited Jerusalem for the Passover. Only John provides for such an earlier visit. For him, Jesus' dramatic intervention was surely of programmatic significance. He was not just another charismatic Galilean healer and teacher, but sent by God to make history.

There follows a very shrewd observation (2:24–25), which drew attention to the phenomenal power of Jesus to read the thoughts and attitudes of everyone that he encountered. This passage underlines John Evangelist's perception that, from the very beginning of his ministry, Jesus had no interest in gathering

---

4. Sayers, *Man Born to Be King*, 273.

5. Robinson, *Priority of John*, 128.

supporters for a political movement. He sought *believers*, with a relationship with him based on deep mutual trust. His kingdom is not "of this world" (18:36).

2:5. The Meeting with Nicodemus (3:1–21)

Nicodemus may have been one of the Jerusalem Pharisees who sought to assess the significance of the religious revival led by John the Baptist. He must have become aware that leadership of the movement was passing to Jesus, and, more recently, that Jesus' ministry had been marked by remarkable events which suggested divine authentication. But Nicodemus was an important member of the religious establishment, and was entwined in its political expedience and compromises. This, of course, is exactly what Jesus means by "the flesh." Nicodemus was indeed a type example of a rich man finding it hard to enter the narrow, needle's eye gate of the kingdom of God, and Jesus had no intention of minimizing his problems.

We are presuming, as Temple does,[6] that John Evangelist was present. Indeed the meeting may well have been in his house. It is obvious that the proceedings were deeply disappointing for John. He would have been sympathetically aware of Nicodemus' difficulties, and that Jesus has set the bar terrifyingly high for him. By the time John writes his gospel, he is unequivocally on the side of Jesus, and cannot bring himself to record the inconsequential end to the actual conversation. Instead he switches to his own spiritual commentary, greatly to the blessing of subsequent Christian readers.

2:6. A Parallel Ministry with John the Baptist (3:22—4:2)

For a time Jesus and his disciples conducted a ministry of preaching in the Judean countryside, calling people to repentance and baptism. The detailed account, and the relative proximity to Jerusalem, suggest that the Evangelist may have been in the party. John

6. Temple, *Readings in St. John's Gospel*, xviii.

the Baptist was similarly engaged at the same time, at Aenon, near Salim, probably in the northern part of Judea. There is no reference to the Jordan, and Aenon means "place of springs." So v. 23 probably refers to the abundance of spring water, feeding ponds and tanks. Due to a change to a drier climate, water tables have fallen greatly through most of the Middle East over the last two thousand years. With people also in abundance, there was scope for both missions, and presumably they arranged to meet. The Evangelist recorded John the Baptist's gracious words (3:27–30), but was then impelled to add his own commentary.

This section supplies the important time indicator (3:24) that John the Baptist had not yet been imprisoned. The Synoptic Gospels are unanimous in dating the beginning of their record of the Galilean ministry of Jesus as after John's imprisonment (Matt 4:12; Mark 1:14; Luke 3:20). We can therefore assume that everything John Evangelist records up to this point refers to an early part of the ministry of Jesus, about which the Synoptic editors had little information. Indeed this may apply to everything up to the end of John chapter 5, for both verses 5:1 and 6:1 refer to the passage of a substantial period of time. The remark recorded in John 4:45 implies that Jesus was not yet widely known in Galilee. Only those who had been with him in Jerusalem knew he was exercising a powerful ministry of preaching and healing. The remark in 7:11–12 confirms that Jesus already had a substantial number of followers in Jerusalem at an early stage of his ministry, something that would not be suspected from study confined to the Synoptic gospels.

2:7. The Conversation with the Samaritan Woman and Its Aftermath (4:3–42)

This encounter, and the long and intricate conversation that sprang out of it, is so remarkable that it could never have been put on record unless it was based on a real event. It is a Johannine classic, replete with detail, even to the time of day. If it had been told by Jesus afterward it would surely have been more concise. We might contrast the account of the temptations of Jesus. The most likely scenario is that John Evangelist remained with Jesus while the Galilean disciples went into the town to buy food. The conversation with the woman is an example of the power of Jesus to know instantly all about a person, which has already been made evident in the case of Nathanael (1:47–51) and in the comment in 2:24–25. It is doubtless the striking theological content of the conversation that led John Evangelist to give it so much space. Jesus is the giver of living water, welling up to eternal life, exactly parallel to the living bread of chapter 6. Worship is not to be localized. This prefigured the theme of Stephen's speech, of which the Evangelist was doubtless aware. But for a young Pharisee, presumably with a sheltered upbringing in a highly respectable family, to see Jesus dealing so confidently with a woman who had a sordid past, without either judgment or compromise, and turning the dross of her situation into a golden outcome would be a mind-blowing experience, with every detail remembered for a lifetime. John would also be aware of the antagonism between Jews and Samaritans (later so well exemplified by John bar Zebedee, as recorded in Luke 9:54–56). He now experienced Jesus reaching out in love to Samaritans, recognizing that they were very much "lost sheep of the house of Israel." This was another aspect of the "steep learning curve" being experienced by John. When he wrote, he would be aware that the immediate evangelical harvest among Samaritans which Jesus greeted so enthusiastically (in words similar to Matt 9:37–38 and Luke 10:2) had continued during the mission described in the eighth chapter of Acts. The comment in 4:37-38 may well be the Evangelist's reflection on this in the light of the use by Jesus in another context of the aphorism, "one sows, another reaps" (cf. Matt 25:24–26).

2:8. Return to Galilee (4:43–54)

After a short stay in Samaria, Jesus and his party completed the journey back to Galilee. John noted that he headed to Cana, not Nazareth or Capernaum. This is possibly a flag which indicates that John was an eyewitness of the healing at a distance of the royal official's son. We notice that both the objective of Jesus (4:48) and the outcome of the healing (4:53) was that people came to believe in him. The loyalty required is again not to a movement or a program, nor even to the kingdom of God, it is to the person of Jesus as God's authentic regent.

Following our scenario, we may presume that the Evangelist's visit to Galilee on this occasion was brief, and that he returned to Jerusalem. The first verse of chapter 5 implies that Jesus remained in Galilee at this point for a substantial time. Some of the events recorded in the Synoptic Gospels presumably occurred during this period, but we note that the Evangelist does not mention them. He was no doubt aware of some or all of them, as he implied at the end of his gospel (20:30; 21:25), but his evident policy was to concentrate on the events of which he had personal experience.

2:9. Healing at the Pool of Bethesda (5:1–47)

In chapter 5 we have an account of a visit made by Jesus to Jerusalem, at the time of a festival, possibly the Feast of Tabernacles. There is no mention of disciples, so there was evidently no substantial accompanying party, and the healing event is not mentioned in any of the other three gospels. As the visit seems to have been short, it may be that Jesus made it while the Twelve were making their preaching tour (Luke 9:1–6). Alternatively, the events of chapter 5 may also predate the calling of the Twelve.

The account of the healing miracle is very circumstantial. The Pool of Bethesda has been excavated. It is big: 330 by 250 ft., with a wide colonnaded veranda all the way round and one across the middle, five therefore in all, just as the gospel says.[7] There were in fact two identical marble-lined pools, each as big as a swimming bath. John says that a great number of disabled people had gathered; indeed there would have been plenty of room for this. We notice that John also knew about conversations of Jesus with the invalid both before and after his healing.

7. Gonen, *Biblical Holy Places*, 160.

The healing took place on the Sabbath. In vv. 16–30, John gives an account of the sequel. Jesus, teaching, presumably in the temple, claimed to be Son of God, and therefore not only exempt from regulations concerning the Sabbath, but also arbiter of the fate of human beings after death. Those that believe that he is who he affirms, and trust themselves to him, will have eternal life. He claimed to be the fulfillment of a prophecy ascribed to Moses in the book of Deuteronomy (18:17–20). Both the claim itself and the scripture presented in support offer stark alternatives to his hearers. The claim is either appalling truth or appalling blasphemy. In the Scripture, the true prophet is to be believed in everything, while the false, presumptuous prophet is to be put to death. Jesus was already a highly contentious person. When people speak of "gentle Jesus, meek and mild," one wonders why anyone would want to put such a man to death. Indeed a selective reading of the Synoptic Gospels might lead to the same thought about a "harmless Jewish rabbi." But the Gospel of John leaves the reader in no doubt that Jesus is either who he says he is or he is completely mistaken and suffering from a very dangerous delusion indeed. These were the alternatives then, and they remain the alternatives today. Contemplating them would have left a loyal, educated Jew, well esteemed within the religious establishment of his day, staring into the abyss. Jesus' claims for himself were incredible, but he was a man of evident integrity who asserted them with utter confidence. John felt in his inmost being that he was telling the truth. But others had already concluded (7:1) that Jesus was totally deluded and deserved the fate of a false prophet.

2:10. The Feeding of the Five Thousand (6:1–24)

Before the events recorded in chapter 6, we have a lapse of time, which might have been anything from several months to a year, depending on which feast is meant in 5:1. Verse 6:1 implies that Jesus had been back in Galilee for some time. The feeding is recorded in all four gospels, but the telltale signs that John Evangelist had returned to Galilee and was actually present are very evident. He alone records that it was near Passover time and that it was a grassy spot, and also, most tellingly, that a boy supplied the food. Even more significantly, he alone is aware that the event ended with a move to make Jesus a revolutionary leader, which was clearly the explanation for his sudden departure. This is also the background for the intense discussion in the latter part of chapter 6, in which Jesus made clear that he is not the Messiah of popular expectation, but God's regent, with power over the eternal destiny of every human being. Among the Synoptic editors, only Mark shows awareness of this outcome, with the cryptic remark that the disciples "had not understood about the loaves; their hearts were hardened" (6:52). But then even he switched to another unrelated pericope. However, John, Mark and Matthew all record how Jesus came to the disciples in the boat, walking on the water. It may be supposed that John Evangelist was with them in the boat, noting the distance they had come (6:19) and the ambiguous use by Jesus of I AM, the name of God.

2:11. The "Bread of Life" Discourse (6:25–71)

Only John records the actual aftermath of the feeding, with his explanation of how "the crowd," i.e., a substantial number of those present there, pursued Jesus, and caught up with him, by this time teaching in the synagogue in Capernaum. Hunter remarked that "only John 6 makes proper sense of the events recorded in Mark 6:30—8:33. . . . The whole sequence of events not only hangs together but preserves a convincing explanation for what must have been a turning point in the ministry."[8]

First of all, Jesus needed to discourage anyone who had come "intending to make him king." But he also needed to make clear to his followers in Galilee what he had already explained in Jerusalem. While concern with material needs is legitimate, such things are subsidiary to accepting him as the One whom God has sent. However, this was no systematic discourse, more like a disorderly

---

8. Hunter, *According to John* (1968 ed.), 44.

discussion. As a result it was sometimes repetitious. To most of those present, the images and analogies Jesus used were incomprehensible. They would certainly have deterred anyone looking for a charismatic political leader. The Evangelist was present, but not as a detached stenographer. He was emotionally involved, and clearly hung on Jesus' words. At times, he was probably almost as baffled as the others, particularly when Jesus spoke of the need to eat his flesh and drink his blood. When John was producing his gospel, the meaning would have been illuminated by the Last Supper, the crucifixion and the resurrection, and, presumably, by experience of the Eucharist. It is to his credit that he abstained from inserting anachronistic comments.[9] Bauckham discusses this passage. He places its main emphasis on the reciprocal indwelling of Jesus and the believer (as in 6:56), a concept echoing the importance Paul gives to being "in Christ." For modern Christians this idea is strongly connected with Holy Communion, by which we are assured that "we are very members incorporate in the mystical body of thy Son."[10] Connected with this is the claim, repeated several times, that Jesus is the sole donor of eternal life. Though life in the Spirit can be a present experience (6:63), the main emphasis is future. Jesus will raise the believer to eternal life "at the last day." The challenge, then and now, is whether or not we believe that Jesus has this God-given authority. For many the response was, and still is, "This is a hard teaching. Who can accept it?" (6:60).

Presumably Jesus, like Gideon, wanted to winnow down his band of disciples to those who were firmly committed to him, and had some understanding of his true nature and the objectives of his mission. In this he succeeded, if Peter indeed spoke for all his closer followers when he testified: "Lord, to whom shall we go? You have the words of eternal life. We have believed and have come to know that you are the Holy One of God." I am sure that Peter spoke for the Evangelist. Sadly, he did not speak for Judas.

9. Bauckham, *Gospel of Glory*, 94–104.

10. Prayer after Communion in the Book of Common Prayer of the Church of England.

2:12. Further Controversy in Jerusalem
(7:1–54; 8:12–59)

About six months elapsed, between March/April (close to Pass-over) to the Feast of Tabernacles in September or October, during which time Jesus remained in Galilee. Nothing is recounted that suggests that the Evangelist was with him during this time, so that John's eventful visit to Galilee probably lasted only a few days. His home was in Jerusalem, and he was not one of the twelve disciples that Jesus had selected for the Galilean ministry.

Just before the Feast of Tabernacles, his brothers suggested that Jesus should accompany them on a visit to Jerusalem. Commentators agree that these were Jesus' natural brothers and not disciples (even though the disciples are called brothers at 20:17, after the resurrection). At this stage the brothers were not "believers," and still supposed that Jesus wanted to be a popular preacher. They were clearly unaware of the hostility he had provoked on his last visit to Jerusalem.[11] Jesus presumably explained to John Evangelist on his eventual arrival why he had not come to Jerusalem at the start of the feast.

Midway through the feast, Jesus began teaching in the temple. He spoke cogently and competently, which surprised his hearers, as he was known to lack formal training. He explained that his teaching comes from God, who sent him. They complained that, on the contrary, he is a lawbreaker because he healed the invalid at the Pool of Bethesda on the Sabbath. Jesus pointed out that if someone can be circumcised on the Sabbath, it is illogical to object to a whole person being healed on the Sabbath.

What follows makes it clear that there had been a move to arrest Jesus, perhaps as a result of what he had said on his previous visit. The intended outcome might have been stoning on a charge of blasphemy. Jesus now repeated his claim to have personal authorization from God, and the temple guards were sent to arrest him. Overawed by the confidence with which Jesus was speaking,

11. Barrett, *Gospel according to St. John*, 310–11; Beasley-Murray, *John*, 106–7.

and perhaps by the number of his supporters, they returned empty handed. The Evangelist's account is complex, probably because he knew both sides of the story. There were the public activities of Jesus and his audience, some of which he may have witnessed, but also the private proceedings of the Sanhedrin and the temple guards, about which John also had information, perhaps through Nicodemus. The mention of "the chief priests and Pharisees" suggests at least an informal committee of the Sanhedrin. This included leading members of the high priest's family, but also some influential Pharisees, such as Nicodemus, and, just possibly, John himself. This might have been so if he was a member of the high priestly family, a possibility to be explored later.

The gospel, as we have it, inserts the episode of the woman taken in adultery here, but this is generally accepted as an interpolation.[12] John's account continues with further controversial teaching, beginning with "I am the Light of the World," in which Jesus once more claimed to be an authoritative mouthpiece of God, his Father. This culminated for the listeners with the final appalling blasphemy, "Before Abraham was, I am." This constituted a claim to be on a level with God. With a summary stoning imminent, Jesus slipped away.

The end of chapter 8 marks a possible juncture when Jesus might have withdrawn from Jerusalem altogether for a few weeks. The next indications of time comes in 10:22, "winter" and "the Feast of Dedication" (usually in December), three months after the Feast of Tabernacles. The imminent threat to his life before "his time had come" is one point in favor of him going elsewhere. Other possible places in the text for an absence from Jerusalem are at the end of chapter 7 and between vv. 21 and 22 of chapter 10. It is obvious that Jesus spent substantial periods in Galilee as well as in Jerusalem, but, presumably John was not with him during these times.

---

12. Beasley-Murray, *John*, 143–44.

2:13. The Healing of the Man Born Blind (9:1–21)

The impressive amount of detail in this section strongly suggests that John was an eyewitness, at least of parts of the story. Was he (or Nicodemus) one of the examining Pharisees, who kept quiet because he was evidently in a minority of one? The treatment of the blind man seems severe, but it is in the context of extreme exasperation with Jesus. This has built up through the lengthy series of controversies recorded in chapters 5 to 8. Jesus was completely undermining the authority of the religious establishment by claiming to speak with the voice of God. Spectacular signs of his authenticity, such as the healing of a man born blind, were likely to lead many people to believe that he was telling the truth. Jesus had sympathizers to protect him, so the authorities vented their feelings on his defenseless client. In this situation, the raising of Lazarus from death will be the "last straw," leading the authorities to throw caution to the winds, and plan actively for the death of Jesus, and maybe Lazarus as well (12:10). Chapter 9 is thus part of a coherent story, and there seems no strong case for regarding it as inserted to reflect conflict between the supposed "Johannine Community" and the local synagogue.

2:14. The Good Shepherd (10:1–21)

This is an interesting passage in that Jesus adopted a style of teaching, with parables and analogies, much closer to that recorded in the Synoptics than that which is characteristic of John. The perceptive comment at the end is a probable explanation. The audience was divided, and not uniformly hostile. Some said, "He is demon possessed and raving mad." Others said, "These are not the sayings of a man possessed by a demon. Can a demon open the eyes of the blind?" The opposed categories of sheep and robbers used by Jesus neatly reflect this division. The detailed account strongly supports the presence of John Evangelist as an eyewitness.

2:15. Escape from a Further Threatened Stoning (10:22–42)

Here Jesus reverted to an uncompromising stance. In the Synoptics, the bitterness of the opposition to Jesus in Jerusalem comes as a surprise, but, in John's account, Jesus' relentless insistence on his divine status evidently raised such fury in his opponents that it is his escape from immediate lynching that is the surprise. However, the threatened stoning was not the time or means appropriate to his inevitable martyrdom, so Jesus left Jerusalem. He went to Peraea (Transjordan), which was under the more relaxed regime of the Tetrarch Philip. Here favorable memories of the ministry of John the Baptist were still fresh, and apparently it was not only in Galilee that John had pointed to Jesus as his successor. As a result Jesus and his message were welcomed, in sharp contrast with the situation in Jerusalem. Jesus may have spent some time here, perhaps most of the three months between the Feast of Dedication and the Passover. During this time he was evidently joined by a group of Galilean disciples (11:7), including some or all of the Twelve (e.g., Thomas in 11:16). In keeping with a diversion to Peraea, Matthew, Mark and Luke all make Jericho a place through which Jesus and his Galilean disciples made their final journey to Jerusalem. Then a messenger comes with news of the serious illness of Lazarus (11:3–4), and perhaps this messenger was John Evangelist in view of the details that follow.

2:16. The Raising of Lazarus (11:1–44)

The failure of the Synoptic gospels to mention this event is a considerable problem that must inevitably be encountered in the course of the exercise being attempted here. Fortunately it has received thorough consideration by Richard Bauckham.[13] His explanation is to propose that the Synoptic editors drew heavily for their account of the Passion on a very early tradition of ca. 40 CE. At this time Christians were being actively persecuted. People, such

13. Bauckham, *Testimony of the Beloved Disciple*, 173–89.

as Nicodemus, Lazarus, Mary and Martha, would be exposed to unnecessary danger if their close association with Jesus was revealed. By the time John Evangelist was writing, this danger was long past, and there was no need to hide their involvement. He tells the story in such intimate detail that its fabrication would be unbelievably cynical. The grief of Martha and Mary, and the way Jesus shared it, is observed with particular tenderness. The most credible explanation is that John was an eyewitness. To his mind, the raising of Lazarus must have been irrefutable proof that Jesus' account of himself was the truth, and that the power of the Creator of the Universe was indeed at his disposal.

2:17. The Plot to Kill Jesus (11:45–57)

Once more Nicodemus was possibly the informant about the proceedings of the meeting of the Sanhedrin which followed. The current high priest, Caiaphas, called for decisive action against Jesus. It is interesting to note that alongside his antipathy to Caiaphas, John has great respect for the office of high priest. He was a welcome visitor to the house of Annas (18:16), Caiaphas's father-in-law and predecessor, and the possibility that he was a relative is discussed by Bauckham.[14]

After the raising of Lazarus, John noted that Jesus and his disciples withdrew to Ephraim, possibly to be identified with a place some fifteen miles north of Jerusalem. Someone, perhaps John, had warned him that his life was in danger, but he had much important teaching still to cover, especially with his disciples. Meantime many of his supporters from Galilee arrived in Jerusalem for the Passover.

2:18. The Anointing in Bethany (12:1–11)

John Evangelist may well have been present. As the Messiah is "the anointed one," the anointing was a significant, even subversive, act. John felt Judas's objection to the expense was particularly

14. Bauckham, *Testimony of the Beloved Disciple*, 37–50.

obnoxious, because Judas had himself misused money from the common stock. Dorothy Sayers had an ingenious scenario explaining his theft.[15] She supposed Judas used the money to bribe the messenger making the arrangements for collecting the colt described in Mark 11:1–2. He then misunderstood the significance of the message. We may be sure that Judas gave himself some worthy reason for all his actions, but John detested his apparent deviousness and disloyalty with particular pungency.

2:19. The "Triumphal Entry" (12:12–19)

"Triumphal" is our word. John realized, as Mark had already done, that the event should be called the Humble Entry, as the context of the quotation from Zechariah (9:9–10) makes clear. The King comes on a donkey to show he is gentle and peaceful, deliberately dispensing with war horses and chariots. Dorothy Sayers has Jesus fulfilling the prophecy by being offered the opportunity of riding either a horse or a donkey, and choosing the donkey. John has the authorities ignoring this coded message. Instead they felt threatened by the large number of people in attendance.

2:20. Concluding Public Ministry (12:20–50)

Constrained by their oversimplified chronological framework, the Synoptic Gospels place much teaching in the temple in the four following days. John was aware that, in actual fact, Jesus sought privacy (12:36), and gave his remaining time almost entirely to his close disciples. This was hard for a group of Greek-speaking Jews, who wanted to meet Jesus, yet the final publicly spoken words of Jesus (12:23–36 and 44–50) are addressed to a worldwide audience, his coming crucifixion will draw all to himself (12:31–34). He had come into the world as a light, so that no one who believes in him will stay in darkness, but will have the opportunity of eternal life (12:50).

15. Sayers, *Man Born to Be King*, 184.

2:21. Jesus Washes His Disciples' Feet (13:1–17)

Jesus had made an arrangement with the owner of a substantial house in Jerusalem that, for two or three days over the Passover celebration, he would make a large guest room available for Jesus and his close disciples. Presumably the Galilean disciples were not well acquainted with the residential part of Jerusalem. Jesus also did not want Judas to know in advance where they were going to be lodged. He wanted to ensure that Judas had no opportunity to give this information to the authorities before Jesus had completed his last session with his disciples. This would explain why Jesus sent Peter and John bar Zebedee at an agreed time to meet the man with a water pot (Mark 14:13–16). Howard Marshall's comments on the equivalent passage in Luke (22:8–12) are significant. The request to the householder to show the room is imperative, on the authority of the Teacher (*ho didaskalos*). Marshall says "the presumption is that the householder was a disciple."[16] That the disciple was John Evangelist is a further presumption made in this work. Doubtless with the help of servants, the disciples prepared the guest room for their stay, together with the special requirements for the Passover meal on the following day.

Everyone then gathered for the evening meal, *deipnon* in Greek. The Evangelist is very clear that this is not the Passover meal, i.e., *pascha*. It would, however, be preceded by the eve of Festival Kiddush. In this, a prayer is said in blessing of a cup of wine, which is then passed round, and after this there is a prayer of blessing over the bread. It is notable that this is the order given by Luke (22:17–20). There might then be another cup of wine at the end of the meal. It should be noted that Luke is ambiguous whether Jesus' eager desire to eat the Passover (Luke 22:15–16) was fulfilled or disappointed. Very early Jewish tradition states that "on the eve of the Passover they hanged Jeshu."[17] This suggests that John is right that the "Last Supper" was not a Passover meal,

16. Marshall, *Gospel of Luke*, 792.

17. Babylonian Talmud, Sanhedrin 43a, as quoted by Beasley-Murray, *John*, 319.

something he would obviously know if, as we suggest, he was the host who entertained Jesus and the other disciples. The Synoptic editors, not being present, seem to have presumed that it was the Passover meal, although they avoid saying so unambiguously.

Although John Evangelist must have been well aware of the origin of the Christian Eucharist, as described by the other Evangelists, he omitted mention of it in favor of the foot washing which they did not record. The impressive detail given, particularly of the interplay with Peter, suggests that John Evangelist was present. If so, his Teacher presumably washed his feet, with the other disciples. The foot washing is an act of immense symbolic importance, which is discussed at length by Bauckham.[18] John is the Evangelist who most emphasizes the awesome greatness of Jesus, the divine associate of the Creator God, but here he emphasizes the humility of Jesus as he undertakes the menial task reserved for a domestic servant. In him indeed, meekness and majesty coexisted.

2:22. Jesus Predicts His Betrayer (13:18–30)

Jesus, the reader of hearts, had long known the risk he had taken by accepting Judas as a disciple (6:70–71). Now he revealed that he knows that Judas is about to betray him to the authorities, something which deeply saddened him, even as it saddened the other disciples. At this point we learn that "the disciple that Jesus loved" was reclining next to him. We assume that he was in this place of honor because he was providing the meal in his own house. If so, while Jesus was the president, John Evangelist was the host. Quietly, Jesus told Judas to go ahead with what he had agreed to do. Thus Jesus remained, at one level, in charge of events, and Judas had to live with the realization that his mistrust of Jesus and his measure of responsibility for his eventual sufferings could not be hidden. Now he went out into the dark, in every sense. Jesus then revealed that there will be a lesser betrayal. Even Peter, the Rock, will wobble in his loyalty.

18. Bauckham, *Testimony of the Beloved Disciple*, 191–206.

2:23. The Farewell Discourse (13:31—16:33)

Jesus knew that organizing his arrest late at night would take time, perhaps three hours, and set about using this time to the full. John's account of his discourse is much longer and more detailed than other parts of the gospel. An attractive explanation, discussed by Beasley-Murray in his Word Biblical Commentary, is that this section began as a separate document of a different genre, that of a *farewell discourse*.[19] It may be suggested that this was put together by the Evangelist, on the basis of his own memories but perhaps in consultation with others present, not long after the death and resurrection of Jesus. Beasley-Murray proposes that 13:31—14:31 was compiled first, and that 15:1—16:33 was added later, as was Jesus' Prayer which now forms chapter 17. Much later, the Evangelist incorporated the discourse into his own gospel. In the meantime, he doubtless used it in his own preaching and teaching. If the First Letter of John is accepted as an example of this, some links are listed by John Stott in an instructive general comparison of themes covered by the letter and the gospel.[20] Through subsequent centuries the three chapters of the Farewell Discourse have been one of the most cherished parts of the Bible. Their exposition deserves a separate book, and D. A. Carson has produced one.[21]

As a result of comparison with teaching recorded in the other gospels, A. M. Hunter concluded:"John is here" (in the Farewell Discourse) "reaching back to a very early form of tradition indeed, and making it the point of departure for his profound theological interpretations; and, further, the oracular sayings which he reports . . . have good claim to represent authentically in substance, if not verbally, what Jesus actually said to his disciples before he went to the Cross."[22] Matthew Black commented: "The rabbinical character of the discourses and their predominantly poetical form certainly

19. Beasley-Murray, *John*, 222–27.

20. Stott, *Letters of John*, 20–28.

21. Carson, *Jesus and His Friends*.

22. Hunter, *According to John*, 114, quoting Dodd, *Historical Tradition in the Fourth Gospel*, 420.

do not discourage the belief that much more of the *ipsissima verba* of Jesus may have been preserved in the Fourth Gospel—with John the Apostle as inspired 'author'—than we have dared believe possible for many years."[23] Their content has indeed telling similarities with the teaching of Jesus in the Synoptic Gospels. They are a sample of his teaching as directed to his close disciples, just as the Sermon on the Mount is a sample of his teaching to a wider audience. It is easy to find analogies with the Synoptic Gospels. For example, the parable of the Vine (15:1–8) is analogous to that of the good and bad fruit trees (Matt 7:16–20). The saying "If anyone loves me, he will obey my teaching" (14:23) is a condensation of the parable of the wise and foolish builders (Matt 7:24–27).

All parts of the Farewell Discourse show clear signs that they have the same author as the rest of John's Gospel, despite the possibility that it had an earlier origin. The literary style is similar. For example, we note John's delight in introducing snatches of conversation into what could have been recorded as an uninterrupted talk by Jesus. The main themes covered are similar in the Farewell Discourse and in the remainder of the gospel. Most notably, both show Jesus having complete intimacy and common purpose with his Father. "It is the Father living in Me who is doing His work." Both show Jesus uncompromising in his demand for total loyalty. "I am the way, the truth and the life. No one comes to the Father except through Me." But, knowing that his disciples were facing a situation of gut-wrenching stress second only to his own, he spoke in a reassuring tone, poles apart from his manner when addressing his opponents. He pictured the importance of maintaining loyalty to him and unity and mutual support among his disciples by using the powerful image of the vine and its branches. He expected the keynote of the Christian community to be love, giving a new commandment. "As I have loved you, so must you love one another. By this all men will know that you are my disciples, that you love one another." Jesus prayed for this in his final great prayer, and John returned to the theme in each of his three letters. How sad that these aspirations have been so poorly fulfilled in Christian history!

23. Black, *Aramaic Approach to the Gospel and Acts*, 151.

2:24. The Great Prayer of Consecration (17:1–26)

Aware that the time for teaching was coming to an end, Jesus turned to prayer. Unlike his prayer in the Garden of Gethsemane, which anticipated the physical agony and spiritual nightmare to come, he looked beyond Calvary to the future. Jesus prayed first for himself (17:1–5), then for his disciples (6–19), and finally for all believers down the ages, including ourselves (20–26). This well-defined structure made the outline of the prayer easier to remember. The occasion and the content of the prayer were alike awesome.

Jesus often prayed in private (e.g., Mark 1:35), but when, occasionally, he prayed in the presence of others, it was partly for their benefit (cf. 11:42). This is supremely so here. We are to think of his departure as returning to the glorious life he had enjoyed with his Father from before creation (cf. Luke 24:26). When we speak of "glory," it denotes a situation which is far beyond the power of any human description. John Evangelist does not record the final disappearance of the earthly Jesus which we call the "Ascension." It is unlikely that he witnessed it. For those who heard the Great Prayer, Jesus did not simply "go up." He resumed the unimaginable status of being one with God, having completed his God-given work. This was, and is, to give eternal life to those whom God has entrusted to him, meaning those who have been enabled to come into a relationship of mutual understanding with Jesus, and so with his Father. For John, this has been the core task of Jesus throughout his ministry, as shown by his words recorded in 6:37–40. The vital importance of a saving relationship with Jesus is always the first concern of John's Gospel.

In vv. 6–19 Jesus prayed for his disciples. Verse 20 indicates that his primary intention in the previous section is for those gathered in the upper room. Now Judas has gone, they are a select group of those who have accepted his message in its entirety. It is the same message that constantly recurs in the teaching recorded in the Gospel of John. The key to everything is confident belief in the divine status of Jesus. "They knew with certainty that I came from you, and they believed that you sent me" (17:8). Total acceptance of his teaching arises from this. Up to now the presence of Jesus has kept them firm in the faith. They are the sheep of the Good Shepherd, and the discussion of this analogy in chapter 10 is about to be very apposite. They will be in the big bad world, and there are self-serving hirelings, thieves and wolves out there. Jesus was exposed to this environment, so his prayer is both powerful and informed. They must cling on to the truths Jesus has revealed to them. His prayer that they should be sanctified means that, while necessarily in the human world, they must remain spiritually set apart from it.

Coming to vv. 20–26, it is wonderful to find Jesus praying for struggling Christians in the twenty-first century. Every reader should apply the prayer to himself (or herself). Jesus' first prayer for us is that we should be in perfect unity. Indeed, amazingly, we should be in the same quintessential unity as that enjoyed by Jesus and his Heavenly Father. This is an awesome standard indeed, and Christians are right to be deeply convicted of sin in this area. As in the parable of the Vine, our perfect one-ness with our fellow Christians is the inevitable consequence of our being united to Christ. Christian disunity is therefore not an option. If we foster it in any way, we are imperiling our relationship with Jesus. We are also spoiling our witness to those outside the Christian fellowship, who should see in us no hostile spirit, but rather a glimpse of divine glory. So the study of church history should bring every Christian to deep repentance. How could it be that Christians whose views differed from the majority were burned alive? Had not the persecutors understood that God willed that weeds among the wheat should be left to his judgment (Matt 13:24–30)? Conversely, Jesus prayed that those who belong to him should be with him forever, sharing his glory and showing love of the same order as that between Jesus and his Heavenly Father. The final reminder is that everything depends on our relationship with God through Jesus.

2:25. The Passion Narrative (Chapters 18 and 19)

All four gospels give systematic accounts of the arrest, judicial examinations and execution of Jesus. Matthew's account is very similar to Mark's. Luke's account adds a few more details. The passion story in John has significant divergences, and has, in some sections, details suggestive of eyewitness testimony. It is contended here that John was a well-liked member of the religious establishment. He made no secret of his loyalty to Jesus, even though it was surely highly deplored. Nevertheless it may be surmised that his family connections made him virtually fireproof, even while he observed most of the proceedings against Jesus. Indeed, when Jesus and the other disciples left his house, perhaps John went to Annas's establishment and heard about the plans for Jesus' arrest.

2:26. The Arrest of Jesus (18:1–12)

It seems possible that John Evangelist went to the Garden of Gethsemane, presumably shadowing, or even accompanying, the hastily assembled arresting party. His account of the arrest is full of circumstantial detail. It is also the record of someone, who, like Jesus, was not surprised by the event. But, unlike the other disciples, he was confident that he was in no danger of arrest himself, and so was able to give a clear account of it. The first detail is that Jesus identified himself with the awesome Name of God, I AM, causing the posse to draw back and fall to the ground in superstitious awe. Then Jesus offered himself for arrest, but asked that his followers should be spared—as they were. Peter, however, brandished a sword, and cut off the right ear of a servant of the high priest. The Evangelist not only knew these details, but even that the name of the servant was Malchus. Jesus' final words, accepting the cup given by his Father, echoed his earlier prayer (Luke 22:42), a prayer which John (not being present) does not record. Presumably John encouraged Peter to accompany him as, at a respectful distance, he followed the posse to Annas's house. I guess Peter discarded his sword in the darkness, and was inwardly churning with fear, even if, as Luke (22:51) records, Jesus had healed the ear.

2:27. The Nocturnal Examination by Annas (18:13–23, 25–27)

Annas was "high priest emeritus." He had been deposed by the Romans in favor of his son-in-law, Caiaphas. The deposition was considered invalid by some, so it was good diplomacy to involve Annas in religious business. The disciple presumed to be John Evangelist was "known" (*gnostos*) to Annas. Barrett considers *gnostos* is likely to mean either a near relative or a close friend.[24] So, he had ready access to Annas's house, and was known to the servants. He was able to bring in his friend Peter, but only as far as the courtyard. John was welcome even in the private rooms, and presumably could listen while Jesus was being interrogated. But this involved leaving Peter completely unsupported in the courtyard. There he was not only assumed to be, like John, a sympathizer with Jesus, but might easily be identified as the man who had just inflicted a serious injury on a fellow servant. To make matters worse still, as Peter thought about it, his action had been futile and highly displeasing to Jesus. He must have been in unimaginable remorse, fear and distress. Jesus would have been well aware of this; there was to be no problem in reinstating a repentant Peter in his love and trust. The Synoptic accounts appear to have Peter going alone, which is a much less compelling background to the story. But their accounts actually imply that he was accompanied by another disciple of Jesus for they recorded the challenge: "you *also* are one of them" (Mark 14:67; Luke 22:58). Incidentally this also indicates that John made no secret of his friendship with Jesus. The Synoptic editors placed Peter's denials in the establishment of Caiaphas, to which Jesus was taken next. It is presumed here that John was better informed, and discreetly corrected this error.

24. Barrett, *Gospel according to St. John*, 525–26.

2:28 The Trial before Caiaphas (18:24)

It is supposed here that John did not have access to the house of Caiaphas, in which Jesus was submitted to a formal, but irregular, trial. The great antipathy of the two men no doubt overrode any family link. Perhaps even Nicodemus was not informed of the trial, given his history as a troublemaker. This is an example of John passing over events, which he clearly knew about, but of which he was not an eyewitness, either at first or second hand.

2:29. The Trial before Pilate (18:28—19:16)

According to Luke, Pilate initially sent Jesus to Herod Antipas. Although Luke is the only authority, this is defended as a real event by Howard Marshall.[25] But, again, it was not accessible to John Evangelist. On the other hand, his very full account of the remainder of the interrogation by Pilate points clearly to his presence. The trial was a public event, and John was a substantial and well-respected person, with no reason to be excluded. He was near enough to Pilate to hear what was said, and perceptive enough to highlight critical points. It was much more than the shouting match pictured by the Synoptic editors, with Jesus largely silent in fulfillment of prophecy (Isa 53:7). It began with the accusation that Jesus is a self-styled king, and hence presumably a revolutionary leader. Pilate established that Jesus was not that kind of "king." The "chief priests and officials" then fell back on the real sentence of the Sanhedrin that "he must die because he claimed to be the Son of God" (19:7). Pilate rejected this as a capital offence, so they "ate crow" and suggested that his claim to be a king of any kind affronts the authority of the Roman emperor. "If you let this man go, you are no friend of Caesar. Anyone who claims to be a king opposes Caesar." Barrett points out that the charge of *majestas*, the equivalent of treason, frequently led to execution in the reign of the Emperor Tiberius.[26] A complaint to him that an instance of treason had been overlooked would have been a real threat to Pilate.

25. Marshall, *Gospel of Luke*, 854–55.
26. Barrett, *Gospel according to St. John*, 543–44.

John Evangelist has thus supplied a much more insightful account of the trial than the Synoptic editors.

2.30. The Crucifixion (19:16–37)

John's outline of events naturally resembles the account in the other gospels, but in detail there are a number of indications of its independence, which was strongly advocated by Dodd.[27] John provided several extra details not mentioned in the Synoptic gospels. He knew that the inscription on the cross was in three languages, and, characteristically, he was aware of the argument about its wording. He could provide details about the division of Jesus' clothing, and even included a snatch of the soldiers' conversation. Only John recorded two words spoken by Jesus just before he died, the first *dipso*—"I thirst"—and then, most significant of all, *tetelestai*—"it is finished." Beasley-Murray is among many commentators noting that the latter could equally be translated "it is accomplished," or even "it is perfected" (the same word root is used in Matt 5:48).[28] What was finished was the work that his Father had sent him to do (cf. John 4:34; 5:36; 17:4), opening the way for the saving and redemption of humankind. Allied to this is the way John described the death of Jesus, "He gave up his spirit." The immortal Son of God voluntarily gave his life for us, as he had explained earlier (10:18).

Only John recorded the piercing of the body of Jesus by a spear, with the issue of blood and water. He accompanied this with a flag of the kind that is assumed here to be a mark that John was an eyewitness. "The man who saw it has given testimony, and his testimony is true. He knows that he tells the truth, and he testifies that you also may believe" (19:35). That this refers to John Evangelist himself is supported by the similarity of the wording here to that in 21:24. John's personal involvement was made even more clear when Jesus entrusted the care of his mother to him, "the disciple whom He loved standing near by" (19:25–27). It is significant that John Evangelist

27. Dodd, *Historical Tradition in the Fourth Gospel*, 121–36.
28. Beasley-Murray, *John*, 352–53.

was the only disciple present who could, "from that hour," take Mary into his own well-appointed home. This same home had presumably been the venue of supper the previous night, and was probably to be the Jerusalem base for all the Galilean disciples including his mother and brothers (Acts 1:13–14), for the next few days. Its location could conceivably be indicated by the tradition that the Coenaculum, the room of the Last Supper, is on Mount Zion.[29] Unlike the Twelve, John was sufficiently confident of his own safety to associate himself with Jesus in this very public way. Notably he was loyal enough to continue to trust him when the truth of his claims was so gravely threatened by events. He had already noted that Jesus is anticipating resurrection (John 16:19–22; cf. 20:8).

2:31. The Burial of Jesus (19:38–42)

It is not unexpected that John Evangelist was well informed about the burial of Jesus by Joseph of Arimathea and his friend, Nicodemus. He recorded that Joseph was a secret disciple of Jesus. Luke mentioned that, like Nicodemus, he was a member of the Sanhedrin, the Jewish governing council. Matthew added that it was Joseph's own tomb, as yet unused, that was provided for Jesus' body. But it is John who knew about the tremendous amount of expensive spices, about seventy-five pounds in weight, brought by Nicodemus. Some have thought this incredible, but it is not so. Such extravagance was a recognition of kingship, on the precedent that five hundred servants had carried sweet spices to the tomb of Herod the Great.[30]

2:32. The Empty Tomb (20:1–18)

It was Mary Magdalene who reported the emptiness of the tomb to Peter and the unnamed disciple, presumably John Evangelist. This would make sense if the close disciples were still staying at John's house. They ran to the tomb. John includes the details of Peter

29. Gonen, *Biblical Holy Places*, 158.
30. Josephus, *Wars of the Jews*, bk. 1, ch. 33, sec. 9, p. 470.

outrunning him, and the position of the cloth that had covered Jesus' head. He remembered this as the "eureka moment" when he felt confident that Jesus had been raised from the dead. Again, only John has the details of the meeting of Jesus with Mary Magdalene, in which Dodd found "something indefinably first hand."[31]

2:33. Two Appearances of the Risen Christ in Jerusalem (20:19–29)

As the first appearance was on the same evening, only three days after the Last Supper, it would cohere with our scenario if both these events took place in John Evangelist's house. Presumably the first appearance is the same as that recorded by Luke (24:36–49). Both begin with Jesus greeting them, saying, "Peace be with you," and showing them his wounds. The accounts then diverge, although, of course, both could be selections from what actually took place. John has Jesus say, "As the Father has sent Me, I am sending you" (cf. Matt 28:19), and inbreathing the Holy Spirit. This echoes prophecies of Jesus expressed in John 14:16–19, which link a resurrection made known only to his disciples with his continuing presence through the indwelling Holy Spirit. We should not think of this inbreathing as anachronistic. The Holy Spirit is eternal, and it is absurd to think of the "Day of Pentecost" as his first appearance on the human scene.

The second appearance was for Thomas's particular benefit. The Evangelist has a special interest in Thomas. He appears four times in his gospel, but elsewhere in the New Testament only in lists of the twelve apostles. Now Thomas sounded the final crescendo in the main text of the gospel: an unequivocal confession of the divinity of Jesus: "My Lord and my God!" This drew from Jesus a wonderful word for the Christians of today: "Blessed are those who have not seen and yet have believed." John's Gospel has indeed played a vital part in bringing many such to faith: we who "believe that Jesus is the Christ, the Son of God, and that by believing . . . have life in His name."

31. Dodd, *Historical Tradition in the Fourth Gospel*, 148.

2:34. The Appendix: Meeting Jesus by the Lakeside
(Chapter 21)

In contrast to some of his predecessors, Bauckham is confident that chapter 21 is by the same author as the remainder of the gospel.[32] This chapter was added to contradict the rumor that Jesus had said that the author would remain alive until his return. The author is identified as "the disciple that Jesus loved" and as "the one who had leaned back against Jesus at the supper and had said 'Lord, who is going to betray you?'" (21:20). The Evangelist is presumably one of the "two other disciples" of v. 2. The "sons of Zebedee," James and John, are also present. It would appear that they are not individually named to avoid confusion of the two Johns by those who knew that the "disciple that Jesus loved" was also called John.

Conversely, it has seemed to some, e.g., Hunter,[33] that the close association of Peter with John, son of Zebedee, which is such a feature of the Synoptics, is strong evidence that he is the John whose future Jesus declined to predict (21:20–24). This argument is largely neutralized in the scenario followed here. It is proposed that John Evangelist and Peter were both members of the original group of five, before the sons of Zebedee became disciples. But, more importantly, it is proposed that it was John Evangelist who had accompanied Peter in the situation that led to his threefold denial, which was now formally expunged by his threefold affirmation of faith. We notice the charcoal fire, recalling the very place where the denials had been uttered.

The Appendix involves an abrupt change of scene to the shores of the Sea of Tiberias. That the resurrected Jesus intended to meet his followers in Galilee is attested by Matthew (28:7) and Mark (16:7). An actual meeting in Galilee was described by Matthew (28:16–20), which is probably the same occasion as Paul reported in his First Letter to the Corinthians (15:6). The command to remain in Jerusalem recorded by Luke (24:49) seems to be problematic, but

32. Bauckham, *Testimony of the Beloved Disciple*, 12.

33. Hunter, *According to John*, 105.

presumably was intended to relate to the period immediately following the decisive parting that we call the "Ascension." It is disappointing that John does not help much to fulfill our natural desire to put the "resurrection appearances" of Jesus into a historical framework. His original intention was clearly to end the gospel with accounts of only three, climaxing with Thomas's great affirmation. By adding a fourth in Galilee, he provided a final "bookend," showing that he shared with Peter an involvement with the ministry of Jesus from the very beginning right to the end. This coheres with the proposition that this gospel is essentially an account of John's eyewitness experience of the words and activities of Jesus Christ.

2:35. Conclusion

The hypothesis offered is that the Evangelist has selected significant events in the ministry of Jesus (including miraculous signs and resurrection appearances) almost exclusively from those at which he was present or about which trustworthy people had given him detailed information. These were mainly located in or near Jerusalem, even though he must have been aware of the extensive ministry of Jesus in Galilee and probably of the contents of one or more of the Synoptic Gospels. He has placed these events, as far as he can, in chronological order, but the connecting framework is minimal. However, John's chronology is invaluable, as William Temple observes. "The Synoptists provide no chronology of the ministry at all until the last week; we do not have to choose between two incompatible chronologies for the Johannine chronology is the only one we have. The Synoptic narrative is unintelligible unless something like the Johannine story is accepted."[34]

John delighted in the challenge of reconstructing whole conversations. This greatly endeared John to Dorothy Sayers when writing her play cycle *The Man Born to Be King*. "It is John who remembers, not only what Jesus said, but what other people said to Him, who can reproduce the cut-and-thrust of controversy

---

34. Temple, *Readings in St. John's Gospel*, xi.

and the development of an argument. . . . Indeed, when John is the authority for any scene, or when John's account is at hand to supplement those of the Synoptists, the playwright's task is easy. . . . And it is frequently John who supplies the reason and meaning of actions and speeches that in the Synoptists appear unexplained and disconnected."[35] It is contended that the reason for these differences is that John Evangelist was actually involved in the events, while the compilers of the other gospels only had a limited supply of secondhand information.

But the Synoptic Gospels are equally complementary to John's Gospel. His record concentrates on the ministry of Jesus in Jerusalem, with only brief snapshots of his Galilean ministry, which may coincide with John's own visits to the area. The Synoptics give a rich account of the teaching and other activities of Jesus in Galilee, alongside their historically distorted account of those in Jerusalem. The explanation for this is surely the same as that given for the limited scope of John's Gospel. It is that the Synoptics too are indirectly based almost entirely on eyewitness material. For the most part, these eyewitnesses had only accompanied Jesus to Jerusalem on his last visit, and so lacked firsthand information about his earlier activities there.

The scenario presented in this book is offered as a respectable way of understanding the gospels, which, necessarily, involves assumptions which cannot be proved. It is for others to reach their own conclusions about these matters, and thinking about them should always be secondary to our personal response to Jesus Christ as the Evangelists depicted him.

---

35. Sayers, *Man Born to Be King*, 34.

PART THREE

HOW DID THE STORY OF JOHN EVANGELIST CONTINUE?

3:1. An Uneasy Relationship with the "Twelve"

UP TO THIS TIME, the story has depended on internal evidence, the narrative in the Gospel of John. Now its continuance must be based on external evidence, which is limited and debatable, so that any conclusions must be considered speculative. For the first two years or so, up to the dramatic changes triggered by the trial and martyrdom of Stephen,[1] some relevant considerations can be deduced from the Gospels and the Acts of the Apostles. In Galilee Jesus had appointed twelve of his disciples to "be with Him, to send them out to preach and to have authority to drive out demons" (Mark 3:14–15). The twelve aspired to a wider authority in the kingdom which Jesus came to inaugurate (Matt 19:27–28; Luke 22:24–30, etc.). Presumably in order to fulfill this role (which included sitting on thrones judging the twelve tribes of Israel), they replaced Judas immediately after the ascension of Jesus (Acts 1:21–26). But, at the "Last Supper," following my hypothesis, it was made very apparent that another John, someone outside the Twelve, stood very high in the esteem of Jesus. His house had become the temporary base of their fellowship (Acts 1:13–14). This is made clear by their return

1. Two years was thought a reasonable estimate by Bruce, *Paul, Apostle of the Free Spirit*, 474.

43

after experiencing the ascension to Jerusalem, not Bethany, and to the upper room where they were staying.

To add to their embarrassment, Peter, their leader, had found that this John was on close terms with Annas, the high priest emeritus, a leading opponent of the Christian cause, who had helped bring about the cruel execution of Jesus. They might even have seen the Evangelist as a spy in their midst. So the Twelve quickly sought other accommodation. They presumably had no property in Jerusalem, but an increasing number of local converts enabled them to form a mutually supporting commune (Acts 2:42–47). They met daily in the temple courts, presumably joined in its worship (3:1), and exercised a healing ministry there. Apart from their devotion to Jesus and his teaching, they continued to behave like other Jews. That this continued for the next thirty years is shown by the observances recorded in Acts 21:20–26. While the leaders of the Jerusalem Church tolerated an almost complete divergence from Jewish practice in the Gentile mission, such tolerance was not exercised in Jerusalem. Their conformity clearly spared them from the ferocious antagonism experienced by Stephen and Paul.

3:2. John Evangelist as a Friend in the Court

John Evangelist was under very different pressures to distance himself from the Christian community. From the perspective of the household of Annas, he had established himself in the entourage of John the Baptist and then as a disciple of Jesus, and thus presumably was regarded as a very useful informant about these significant and possibly threatening religious movements. No doubt they were aware that he had been genuinely attracted to Jesus. But now both these leaders were dead, so it would be presumed that John would resume his role as a member of the high priestly family, and would be available for official duties as required.

At this point, it is appropriate to consider the evidence of a letter written toward the end of the second century by Polycrates, Bishop of Ephesus, to Victor of Rome, and quoted by Eusebius. "In Asia great luminaries have fallen asleep." . . . Philip and "John too, he who leaned back on the Lord's breast, who was a priest, wearing the *petalon*, both *martys* and teacher."[2] The *petalon* was a gold plate inscribed with the name of God, worn only by the high priest and only when on duty in the temple.[3] It is hard to believe that John Evangelist ever acted as high priest in services of the temple, but it is possible that the idea arose from a tradition that he was a member of the high priestly family. John of Ephesus is not otherwise known as a martyr, so *martys* presumably carries the alternative meaning of witness. This may well refer to his witness to the person and earthly life of Jesus, culminating in his authorship of the gospel. Richard Bauckham discussed Polycrates's words in conjunction with Acts 4:5–7.[4] He mentions speculation that John Evangelist is the John listed there as a member of the high priest's family, together with Annas, Caiaphas and Alexander. John was a common name among Jews at that time, but there is no evidence that there was a high priest called John during the relevant period. Nevertheless, if Polycrates's statement was an exaggeration of a genuine memory that John was a member of the high priest's family, it coheres with Luke's observation that "a large number of priests became obedient to the faith" (Acts 6:7). This may also be an exaggeration, but presumably had some factual basis. So, while it seems a bizarre coincidence that John Evangelist should be a member of a judicial tribunal examining John bar Zebedee and Peter, it is not inconceivable. His suitability could have been argued on the ground that he was the expert on the "Jesus Movement" in the high priest's family. Annas and Caiaphas would certainly be unaware how close had been his involvement with the defendants! It would even be possible to extend the speculation to suppose that John Evangelist might be included among the "associates" of the high priest who imprisoned Peter and John (Acts 5:17–18), and that he was the mysterious "insider" who engineered their release. What is objective fact is that, when Luke was seeking the information which he used in the Acts of the Apostles, the Christian community could supply abundant details about the proceedings of

2. Lawlor and Oulton, *Eusebius*, 1:169.

3. Bauckham, *Testimony of the Beloved Disciple*, 37.

4. Ibid., 48.

the Sanhedrin and the high priestly tribunal up to the death of Stephen. The details in Acts (4:15–17; 5:21–26, 33–40; 6:13—7:53) all seem to refer to private meetings. But there is almost nothing in Acts about their later activity. As organizers of a great persecution, this later activity must have been considerable, yet Saul appears to be the only informant about it, in marked contrast with the earlier period.

3:3. Stephen's Speech (Acts 7)

The last episode in this period that Luke recorded in detail in Acts was the speech that Stephen made in his defense. This record is so detailed that it could hardly have been made by a hostile person who was deeply involved emotionally, such as Saul. In his exasperation he could hardly have remembered the steps in Stephen's carefully crafted argument, but its style is very reminiscent of the detailed way in which John Evangelist reported speeches and discussions. Howard Marshall pointed out that "the speech of Stephen has by no means been fully assimilated to Lucan ideas, but retains several individual characteristics."[5] A. E. Harvey also noticed that "it contains a number of words and idioms which are unusual for Luke, and suggests that he may have been drawing on some source rather than composing freely as he went along."[6] The observer, from whose memory and/or notes the source derives, must have had a formidable acquaintance with the Old Testament, and have been to some extent emotionally detached. As the episode began as formal judicial proceedings, might he not even have been acting as minuting secretary? If the scenario explored in this booklet is accepted, John Evangelist is a strong candidate to be the channel through which the account of Stephen's speech reached the Christian community in Jerusalem.

What of the content of the speech? Here Harvey's exposition is masterly, and points out that it completely reverses the scriptural commendation both of the Mosaic law in its written form and of

5. Marshall, *Luke—Historian and Theologian*, 72.
6. Harvey, *Companion to the New Testament*, 211.

the concentration of worship in the temple.[7] So far from accepting and zealously seeking to apply God's law as revealed through Moses, in its true form, as "living words," the Jews had rejected it. Instead of the simple code of the "Ten Commandments," or better still the fundamental guidelines of loving God and loving neighbor, they had elaborated it into an elaborate and very burdensome rule book. The temple, first built by Solomon, was, from the beginning, a mistake, because "the Most High does not live in houses made by men." Stephen then quoted Isaiah (66:1–2), 'Heaven is my throne, and the earth is my footstool. What kind of house will you build for me? says the Lord. Or where will my resting place be? Has not my hand made all these things?' But you persecuted the prophets, and killed those who predicted the coming of the Righteous One. And now you have betrayed and murdered him—you who have received the law that was put into effect through angels, but have not obeyed it" (Acts 7:52–53).

At a stroke, Stephen rubbished the twin pillars of contemporary Judaism, Torah and Temple, and threatened to put both rabbi and priest out of business. He surely expected the intense fury of an audience largely composed of these professionals. There was no room left for the gentle "wait and see" advice of Gamaliel (Acts 5:35–40), or for toleration of a Christian sympathizer in a high priestly household.

3:4. The Effects of Stephen's Speech

In the Acts, Luke records the stoning of Stephen, with echoes of the crucifixion of Jesus in his prayer for the forgiveness of the killers. This is followed by his vision of reception into glory by Jesus, who is given the title of Son of Man in the sense of Daniel chapter 7. He continues with the persecution which followed, and the departure of many Christians into exile. The Twelve remained, showing great bravery, but also, no doubt, insisting on their status as loyal Jews.

7. Ibid., 408–11.

The position of John Evangelist, if indeed he had remained as a known Christian sympathizer within the household of Annas, would have become completely untenable. He was presumably well aware that Jesus deplored the development of a relatively simple Mosaic Code, summarized in the Ten Commandments (or better still in the twin principles of loving God and our fellows), into a burdensome legal rule book. He was certainly aware that Jesus foresaw that God would be worshipped everywhere in spirit and truth, with no focus on Jerusalem (John 4:21–24). John possibly saw that something like Stephen's narrative was necessary if God's self revelation to the Jews was to be developed into a faith for all people. But this could take no root in Jerusalem at this time. The best John could hope for was that his kinsmen would turn a blind eye until he was safely out of Judaea. Where he spent the early years of his exile is completely unknown. But he would have exchanged a life at the center of Jewish affairs in Jerusalem for one in a very diverse Greek-speaking culture with a small, but growing Christian minority. Within the Christian community his personal experiences of Jesus would have been greatly valued, and John Stott argued strongly that the Johannine letters contain evidence of this.[8] But, apparently, a full report of his experiences was not circulated in writing for some years, with the possible exception of his account of the Farewell Discourses. Clearly in composing his gospel, John would have been aware of the circumstances of his local Christian community, although a vivid recreation of the historical Jesus Christ was his principal objective.

For the remaining members of the Jerusalem church, John's involvement with their story would have been very hard to understand, and so best forgotten. When Luke was gathering information about the early days of the Jerusalem church some thirty years later, before he wrote the Acts of the Apostles, all he gleaned was that there had been members of the priestly family who were sympathetic to the Christian cause. Only later still, when John had become a much loved Christian leader who was one of the last

8. Stott, *Letters of John*, 30–44.

surviving eyewitnesses of the earthly life of Jesus, did his friends persuade him to compose his gospel.

3:5. The End of the Story

Latterly, it appears that John the Evangelist lived in Ephesus, which is the traditional place where the Gospel of John was written. Irenaeus, Bishop of Lyons in the last quarter of the second century, wrote: "John, the disciple of the Lord, who leaned on His breast, also published the gospel while living at Ephesus in Asia."[9] In a largely Gentile environment after 70 CE the story of Jesus remained luminously relevant. Unfortunately for us, the background of John's own early life in the religious establishment of a Jerusalem that had entirely disappeared would have seemed of little continuing relevance. Indeed it would have been completely incomprehensible to his fellow Christians.

If, as seems likely, John the Evangelist was also the author of the three biblical letters of John, his local ministry was focused on contemporary concerns. However, Marshall and Harvey are among many authors who find insuperable difficulties in believing that he wrote the book of Revelation, despite its connection with the province of Asia.[10] The style of Greek in the gospel and letters is similar, but in Revelation it is completely different. Bauckham supposes John the Evangelist to be the same as John the Elder, mentioned by Papias, and probably the John listed by the *Apostolic Constitutions* as the second bishop of Ephesus, in succession to Timothy.[11] John Stott points out that the letters of John reflect a confidence in the author's authority that would be appropriate in someone who had a living link with Jesus.[12] John's gentler side is reflected in a story of Jerome about his last words, "Little children,

9. Irenaeus, *Adversus Haereses*, 3.1.1–2, as translated in Beasley-Murray, *John*, lxvi.

10. Marshall, *New Testament Theology*, 370; Harvey, *Companion to the New Testament*, 785.

11. Bauckham, *Testimony of the Beloved Disciple*, 50.

12. Stott, *Letters of John*, 37–39.

love one another," which he repeated again and again. When he was asked if that was all he had to say, he replied "It is enough, for it is the Lord's command."[13]

John's reputed tomb in the crypt of the ruined Church of St. John remains a place of pilgrimage.[14] But his real memorial is his gospel, and, probably, the three letters, which so evidently breathe the spirit of those reputed last words: "Little children, love one another."

13. Quoted from Barclay, *Gospel of John*, 1:18.
14. Gonen, *Biblical Holy Places*, 266–67.

PART FOUR

THE "BELOVED DISCIPLE"

A Witness to the Supreme Importance of a Personal Relationship with Jesus Christ

4:1. Introduction

USING THE PHRASE "THE disciple whom Jesus loved" as a description of the author is an indication of his belief that relationship with Jesus is an essential part of the Christian's salvation journey. From first to last the gospel emphasizes the importance of "believing in Jesus," i.e., believing that his account of his relationship with God is true, with the corollary that everything he says is totally reliable. In the New International Version of the Gospel of John there are eighty-six references to the word "believe" and cognates, of which all but three or four relate to belief in Jesus. In the other three gospels combined there are only thirty-seven references to believing, of which seventeen are in contexts other than belief in Jesus.[1] Clearly, belief that what Jesus says is trustworthy is a key precursor to establishing a relationship with Jesus. This emphasis is in keeping with John's declared object in writing: that we "may believe that Jesus is the Christ, the Son of God, and that by believing you may have life in His name" (20:31).

---

1. Author's count from entries in Goodrick and Kohlenberger, *NIV Complete Concordance.*

At the beginning of the gospel there is a detailed description of how Jesus initiated friendships with some of those who became disciples. At the end, two of these friends were charged to continue to follow him devotedly after his earthly presence was withdrawn. All that lies between confirms that the distinctive and dominant feature of John's character and life was his love relationship with Jesus. Indeed a predominant theme throughout John's Gospel and his First Letter is that all relationships should be characterized by love. The special Christian word for love—*agape*—is used in them more often than in any other book in the Bible. Jesus and God, his Father, are bound together by indissoluble love. All God's dealings with humankind spring from love, and this is supremely shown in sending Jesus to open a way of salvation (3:16). This way, as described in 17:6–8, is through relationship with Jesus.

4:2. Relationship with Jesus, as Mapped Out in John's Gospel

So John's Gospel emphasizes the importance of relationship with Jesus from first to last. At the beginning it promises to all who receive Jesus, who believe in his name, that is those who recognize who he really is, the right to become children of God. In the human analogies we have to use, this makes Jesus our brother. At the end of the gospel, we have a demonstration of the resilience of the relationship, as the mutual love and loyalty between Peter and Jesus is restored.

Throughout the gospel there are illustrations of stages in the development of relationships with Jesus. He may call an individual, as with Philip (1:43). He may make a general invitation as when he said, "I am the light of the world, whoever follows me will not walk in darkness, but have the light of life" (8:12). After responding to the call, those who have faith in him (2:11), and respond in love and obedience (14:23), have fellowship with God (14:6–7), receive guidance (16:13–14), and find the way to eternal life (e.g., 10:28), albeit through difficulties (16:33). The commitment is lifelong

(11:16), and the full consummation lies beyond physical death (14:2; 17:24).

The offer of relationship with Jesus is universal. He extended it warmly to all who were marginal to contemporary society. He included women, such as Mary of Bethany, Mary Magdalene and the woman at the well, who was also a Samaritan, and the disabled, such as the man born blind (9:35–38). He prepared the way for people, like ourselves, who live long after his earthly visit, to feel welcome as his brethren, by praying for us (17:20–21). Indeed he gave a special blessing to us, who have not seen, but nevertheless have believed in him (20:29).

4:3. Friendship with Jesus

The Gospel of John offers believers a special relationship with Jesus that is described as friendship (*philos*). Like *agape*, *philos* is a word for love, but is often preferred when people are joined by common interests and objectives. Jesus explained what is special about Christian friends (*philoi*) during his last discourse (15:14–17). For a Christian, love is extended widely. But a wise Christian does not fully share his private business with everyone he encounters. He will extend loving concern to some who could not be trusted with confidential information. It is only with a few friends, who are tried and trusted people, that he will share all his knowledge and opinions. Those who were described as the *friends* of the Roman emperor were a chosen group of confidential advisors, with constant access to him. In 19:12, Pilate is told that he cannot aspire to being a friend of the emperor if he releases Jesus. In a quite different context, Abraham was described as the friend of God (2 Chr 20:7; Isa 41:8; Jas 2:23). What lies behind this description is made clear in Genesis 18:17–33, where God discusses with Abraham his response to the evils of Sodom. Abraham was trusted enough for God to share with him the rationale behind his actions.

So Jesus says to his disciples: "I no longer call you servants, because a servant does not know his master's business. Instead I have called you friends, for everything that I have learned from my Father I have made known to you." Study of the Gospel of John is a good way of increasing our knowledge of Jesus. But we find that following Jesus is not a rule book religion, such as that of the Pharisees, with their scrupulous adherence to the Torah. It is a way of life guided by love of God and of our fellows.

John Evangelist greatly cherished his especially warm friendship with Jesus, which is no doubt why he liked to be known as "the disciple that Jesus loved." Much of the first chapter of his gospel is a description of Jesus initiating friendships, including perhaps with John himself. The last chapter shows Jesus affirming that his friendship with John Evangelist is secure throughout time and into eternity, and also reestablishing the damaged friendship with Peter. But you don't have to be one of the inner circle to be a friend of Jesus. Jesus called Lazarus his friend, and went to the length of raising him from the dead. Conversely, he affirmed that "greater love has no one than this, he lay down his life for his friends" (15:13), and that is exactly how he showed his love for us. That love was not only shown on Good Friday, but binds us to him for eternity. We have only to ask for the blessings offered in the prayer of Jesus for his friends recorded in chapter 17 of John's Gospel. Jesus said, "Righteous Father . . . I have made you known to them, and will continue to make you known in order that the love you have for me may be in them, and that I myself may be in them." If we accept that Jesus is indissolubly linked to the supreme Creator God, being offered friendship with Jesus is a truly mind-blowing privilege. It enables us to say with Charles Wesley: "Jesus is our brother now, and God is all our own."[2]

Perhaps the hardest part of being a friend of Jesus is to come to terms with the fact that Jesus has millions of other friends. In our home we keep a card on the mantelpiece reading, "We do not always get to choose our fellow disciples." There is a line in one of Charles Wesley's hymns which reads, "Inseparably joined in heart the friends of Jesus are."[3] Making this true can be far from easy, especially for those we find unlikable, but Jesus' prayer in John

2. Hymn 134 in *Methodist Hymnbook*.
3. Hymn 807 in *Methodist Hymnbook*.

chapter 17 commits us to extend the limits of our love for fellow Christians as widely as is practicable.

4:4. The Consummation of Relationship with Jesus

In his Farewell Discourse, Jesus described the spiritual result of our love for him (14:23–26). In this passage the Revised English Bible seems closest to the original.[4] "Anyone who loves me will heed what I say; then my Father will love him, and we will come to him and make our dwelling with him." Jesus then said that, after his departure, "the advocate, the Holy Spirit, whom the Father will send in my name, will teach you everything, and remind you of all that I have told you." So Jesus promises that if we love him, we will "keep his words" (the literal translation), and then God in all his fullness, Father, Son and Holy Spirit, will actually live within us. This is truly a mind-bending promise, and living appropriately is a lifelong challenge. But there is more. On the same condition, Jesus said, "If anyone keeps my word, he will never see death" (8:51). Jesus has the key to eternal life, and the "word" which unlocks it is not a legal code but love of Jesus based on recognition of who he really is.

4. Revised English Bible (1989).

PART FIVE

A PERSONAL POSTSCRIPT

5:1. The Gospel of John in My Own Life

JOHN EVANGELIST WROTE A powerful account of the life of Jesus Christ, and nested within it the story of the most important part of his own life. But his aim was to transform the life of his readers. He wrote that we might believe that Jesus is the Christ, the Son of God, and that by believing have life in his name. Indeed John Evangelist and his gospel brought me this supreme gift, and they have since touched my life at several critical points.

I was brought up with a brother, named John, three years younger than myself, and we did everything together. When I was thirteen, John suddenly became very ill, and was taken to hospital. I prayed desperately for his recovery. I thought the effectiveness of my prayers would be increased if I read the Bible. I believe the Holy Spirit prompted me to begin by reading the Gospel of John. I reached v. 23 of chapter 14. I read (in the King James' Bible that my lay preacher grandfather, Eno Clark, had given me): "If a man love Me, he will keep My words, and My Father will love him, and we will come to him, and make our abode with him." I knew that I had to pray that this would be true for me, and I believe I have been "in Christ" since that time. However, three weeks from being taken ill, my brother died. He had tubercular meningitis, and, in 1946, there was no possibility of any other outcome. We were all given X-rays, and my father, who was a chemistry teacher and a lay preacher, was found to have pulmonary tuberculosis. He was taken to a sanatorium forty miles away. After several years he recovered, but meantime my mother and I were left on our own. She was emotionally shattered, but, providentially, I was taken in hand by loving Christian grandparents. Strangely, I do not remember questioning my faith because my prayers had not had the desired outcome.

When I was sixteen, my best friend, a brilliant mathematician, had a vacation job with an aerospace company. They were immensely impressed by his work on the trajectory of guided missiles, and he was offered university sponsorship and guaranteed employment.

God clearly spoke to me that, in contrast, I must devote my life for the benefit of humanity and not for destruction. But how? The answer came in a geography lesson when a much-respected Christian teacher described the succession of soils in Russia from the tundra through forest and steppe to the deserts of Central Asia. I became absolutely convinced that God's way for me was to become a soil scientist. This conviction has been confirmed by the providential opportunities that have opened for me. The first was the award of an exhibition (a lesser scholarship) at the College of St. John the Evangelist, in the University of Cambridge. This gave me the ideal academic preparation: a science degree in chemistry, geology and mineralogy, followed by a diploma in agricultural science, specializing in soil science. The college was founded as a Church of England religious confraternity, with a large chapel, where, although already a local preacher attending the Methodist church on Sunday mornings, I also attended evensong and early morning Communion. Before I left, the chaplain told me I would now always be a member of the College of St. John the Evangelist.

On leaving Cambridge, I was for eight years a scientific officer on the staff of the historic Rothamsted Experimental Station, engaged in making soil maps, and then for five years a lecturer in soil science at the University of Aberdeen. I was seconded for a year to the University of Malaya, where I joined with Tim Whitmore, a Christian friend who had been a fellow student at St. John's

College, in studying the soils of tropical rain forests. On the way back from Malaysia, I visited the United States, where I had been invited to lecture in the University of North Carolina and in the Federal Department of Agriculture in Washington. There I was entertained to lunch in the Pentagon dining room by the director, Charles Kellogg. Years later, I had the joy of being assured by Professor Peter Ashton, the director of the Harvard Arboretum, that "your work on tropical rain forest soils has stood the test of time."

From 1969 I moved to become senior lecturer in soil science at Wye College, part of the University of London. In 1977, with the permission of Archbishop Coggan, my wife, Wendy, and I were the first Methodist local preachers to be also licensed as lay readers in the Church of England. On reaching the age of sixty, I "candidated" for ordination as a non-stipendiary Methodist minister. It happened that I attended a seminar at which our district chairman, the equivalent of a bishop, spoke about recent scholarly work on the gospels. In discussion I drew attention to Jesus' saying that everyone who hears his words and puts them into practice is like a wise man who builds on the rock. For a Christian, it is therefore essential that his words are ascertainable. The church has always said that these words are those contained in the four gospels, Matthew, Mark, Luke, and John, and no others. Once we depart from this, all is shifting sand. The chairman's reply was that we could not be sure what Jesus had said, and that this uncertainty applied particularly to words recorded in the Gospel of John. I felt strongly that this view undermined the whole basis of my becoming a Christian.

At the final interview of the "candidating" process, I was asked about the books I had been reading. I mentioned with approval *John—Evangelist and Interpreter*, by Stephen Smalley, and reiterated the argument given above. A few days later I received a letter rejecting my candidature. The only reason given was that the panel had found that I was "too fixed in my opinions to be molded in the course of ministerial formation."

The last paragraph of Smalley's book, which is a quotation from E. M. Sidebottom, sums up splendidly the viewpoint for which I contended. "We can and should listen *in full* to the Johannine interpretation of Christianity. Because it is historically grounded, it is not to be dismissed as an eccentric spin-off from the mainstream; and because it is theologically sophisticated it is not to be ignored as an unacceptable variant of the Jerusalem gospel. We need John in the New Testament . . . for in John we have an unexpectedly traditional evangelist and an unusually perceptive interpreter."[1]

5:2. The Gospel of John Continues Its Evangelical Work

In 2014, the British Universities and Colleges Christian Fellowship launched a project to encourage students to read and study the Gospel of John, as part of their outreach. Under the title "Uncover John," 110,000 copies of the gospel have been distributed, together with 28,000 sets of six studies based on the gospel. Evangelism linked to the "Uncover John" initiative has led hundreds of students to faith in Jesus Christ. So where the gospel is recognized as authoritative, the declared aim of John's Gospel continues to be fulfilled today. But, for many, it has been impeded by the work of critical scholars, and the confused babel of improbable ideas which they have lately propounded.

5:3. The Eagle Returns

Throughout my time in Aberdeen, I was leader of the senior group (aged sixteen upwards) of the Aberdeen Crusader Bible Class, and in the Easter holidays we used to "camp" in a disused railway station at Nethybridge, which had been converted into a small youth hostel. The high spot of our stay was to see the only pair of ospreys then breeding in Scotland, which nested on an island in Loch Garten, very near to the hostel. Some spent hours in the "hide" with their binoculars. The osprey is a fish eagle, a very big bird with a wing span of up to five and a half feet. Like all eagles, it has terrifying talons and a very sharp beak. After ospreys had been extinct in

---

1. Smalley, *John—Evangelist and Interpreter*, 252.

Scotland for forty years, the pair had returned in 1954, and their return was national news.

Appropriately, the traditional symbol of the Gospel of John is an eagle. The prehistory of the idea goes back to the living creatures that were part of Ezekiel's vision of God. Each of these had four faces (Ezek 1:10), of a man, a lion, an ox, and an eagle. The same four creatures appear in the vision of God's throne in Revelation 4:6–8. The idea that they could appropriately stand for Christ originated with Irenaeus of Lyons (ca. 130–202). Christ came as a man, as a lion with royal power, as an ox for sacrifice, and as a flying eagle, bringing the all-powerful Spirit hovering on his wings over the church. Irenaeus then assigned the creatures to the four gospels: the man to Matthew, the eagle to Mark, the ox to Luke, and the lion to John.[2] It was Augustine of Hippo (354–430) who gave the lion to Mark and the eagle to John. This final assignment seems highly appropriate. The eagle is fiercely uncompromising, as is John's insistence that Jesus was uniquely one with God the Father. The eagle is supremely equipped for grasping, as is John's Gospel is equipped for drawing people to faith and salvation. We treat an eagle with the greatest respect.

In contrast, it seems to me that the modern symbol for the Gospel of John might be a parrot, and a caged parrot at that. The gospel's claim to be an eyewitness account of the life of Jesus has been considered improbable, and not to be taken seriously. Many have supposed it was compiled by a committee (representing "the Johannine community"), who were remote from the events, and had a distinctive agenda, perhaps even anti-Semitic. As a result, the whole purpose of the gospel, which is to lead people toward faith in Jesus, and so to eternal life, has been prejudiced. But let us now rejoice! The eagle, which was thought to be extinct for a generation, has returned!

---

2. Irenaeus, *Adversus Haereses*, 3.11.8.

BIBLIOGRAPHY

Barclay, William. *The Gospel of John*. Rev. ed. 2 vols. Daily Study Bible. Edinburgh: St. Andrew, 1975.

Barrett, C. K. *The Gospel according to St. John: An Introduction with Commentary and Notes on the Greek Text*. 2nd ed. London: SPCK, 1978.

Bauckham, Richard. *Gospel of Glory: Major Themes in Johannine Theology*. Grand Rapids: Baker Academic, 2015.

————. *Jesus and the Eyewitnesses: The Gospels as Eyewitness Testimony*. Grand Rapids: Eerdmans, 2006; 2nd ed., 2017.

————. *The Testimony of the Beloved Disciple: Narrative, History and Theology in the Gospel of John*. Grand Rapids: Baker Academic, 2007.

Beasley-Murray, George R. *John*. Word Biblical Commentary 36. Waco, TX: Word, 1987.

Black, Matthew. *An Aramaic Approach to the Gospel and Acts*. Oxford: Oxford University Press, 1967.

Brownrigg, Ronald. *Who's Who in the New Testament*. Paperback ed. London: Dent, 1993.

Bruce. F. F. *Paul, Apostle of the Free Spirit*. Exeter, UK: Paternoster, 1977.

Carson, D. A. *The Gospel according to John*. Leicester, UK: InterVarsity, 1991.

————. *Jesus and His Friends*. Leicester, UK: InterVarsity, 1986.

Dodd, C. H. *Historical Tradition in the Fourth Gospel*. Cambridge: Cambridge University Press, 1963.

Edwards, Ruth B. *Discovering John*. London: SPCK, 2003; 2nd ed., 2014.

Gonen, Rivka. *Biblical Holy Places: An Illustrated Guide*. London: Black, 1987.

Goodrick, Edward W., and John R. Kohlenberger. *The NIV Complete Concordance*. London: Hodder & Stoughton, 1983.

Harvey, A. E. *A Companion to the New Testament*. 2nd ed. Cambridge: Cambridge University Press, 2004.

Hengel, Martin. *The Johannine Question*. London: SCM, 1989.

Hunter, A. M. *According to John*. London: SCM, 1968.

Irenaeus. *Adversus Haereses* 3.11.8.

Josephus, Flavius. *The Wars of the Jews*. Translated by William Whiston. Edinburgh: Nimmo, n.d. (ca. 1878).

Lawler, H. J., and J. E. L. Oulton. *Eusebius, Bishop of Caesarea: The Ecclesiastical History and Martyrs of Palestine*. London: SPCK, 1927.

Marshall, I. Howard. *The Gospel of Luke: A Commentary on the Greek Text*. Exeter, UK: Paternoster, 1978.

————. *Luke—Historian and Theologian*. Paperback ed. Exeter, UK: Paternoster, 1979.

————. *New Testament Theology*. Downers Grove: IVP Academic, 2004.

Methodist Conference Office. *The Methodist Hymn Book*. London, 1933.

Milne, Bruce. *The Message of John*. Leicester, UK: InterVarsity, 1993.

Robinson, J. A. T. *The Priority of John*. London: SCM, 1985.

Sayers, Dorothy. *The Man Born to Be King*. London: Gollancz, 1943.

Smalley, Stephen. *John—Evangelist and Interpreter*. Paperback ed. Exeter, UK: Paternoster, 1983.

Stott, John R. W. *The Letters of John*. Tyndale New Testament Commentaries. 2nd ed. Leicester, UK: InterVarsity, 1988.

Temple, William. *Readings in St. John's Gospel*. First Series. London: Macmillan, 1938.

Vermes, Geza. *The Changing Faces of Jesus*. London: Lane, 2000.